Pastor/poet laurea
collection of poem
voice of God in daily life. Threaded throughout by
images of C.S. Lewis' beloved Aslan, Greg guides us
on a safari of Godwinks, pointing out His quiet
breath in the rustling of the ordinary, bowing before
the divine roars in the disguised majesty of the
everyday. Playful, earnest, observant, the poems
lead the willing reader toward devotion, a slow
prowl toward prayer, stalking elusive glory in the
middle of our most familiar routines.

- Jeff Reed, Pastor, Highland Covenant Church,
Bellevue, Washington

I smiled, wondering if God was toying with us ...
author Greg and me. The Almighty does that, you
know ... just to let us know He's taking part in our
conversations. That thought came to mind as I read
Pastor Greg's delightful poem in these pages,
When God Speaks. My first book was *When God
Winks*. How godwinky is that?

Yet as much as I enjoyed every poem in this sweet
volume, my favorite is *A Godwink Defined*. Especially
Greg's charming line about "dusting for God's
fingerprints."

- SQuire Rushnell
Author, Godwink™ book series

For the past 30 years I have given tours of C.S. Lewis' home, The Kilns. I have been privileged to hear countless stories people have shared about how Lewis influenced their lives. In this book, we follow Greg's unique and thoughtful journey with Lewis. Brilliant!

- Kim Gilnett, United Kingdom Kilns Board Member, C.S. Lewis Foundation

Thank you, Greg Asimakoupoulos, for your personal gift to this reader. I applaud your desire to hear Aslan's voice. As you know, my husband David and I continue to find great joy "hunting for God" in the ordinary events of everyday life.

- Karen Burton Mains Author, *The God Hunt*

I've known Greg Asimakoupoulos for over 40 years. I've admired his outgoing optimism and love for God and people. Greg is unabashed in his joy of life and it is readily revealed in his poetry. His lines of verse speak to me as I, along with Greg, seek God, both in His Word, and in the amazing world we live in. I am honored that he asked to use one of my paintings for the cover of this book.

- Greg Beecham, Wildlife artist

fa Ted &
Carol

when **God** *speaks*

Listening for Aslan in everyday life

Aslan is on the move!

Pastor Greg

when God *speaks*

Listening for Aslan in everyday life

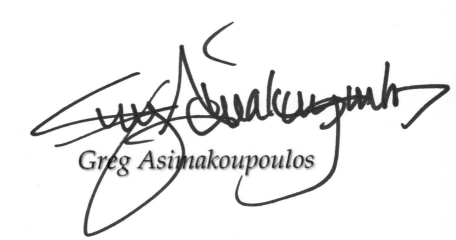

Greg Asimakoupoulos

When God Speaks: Listening for Aslan in everyday life
Copyright © 2021 by Greg Asimakoupoulos

Printed in the United States of America.
ISBN: 978-1-7369703-4-8

Cover: *The Warrior King* by Greg Beecham, used by permission
Cover and interior design: Rick Lindholtz for On the Tracks Media

On the Tracks Media LLC
onthetracksmedia.com

10   9   8   7   6   5   4   3   2   1

Dedicated to my granddaughters, Immy and Ivy,
who continually keep their Papou alert
to the wonders of being a child of God!

An Author's Wish

 May your God-seeking life
be enriched as you read
where the essence of real wealth is found:
in the truths of God's Word,
in the winks of God's grace
and where whispers of Godspeak abound.

Acknowledgements

I am grateful to David and Karen Mains, who were the first to introduce me to the concept of listening to and looking for God in everyday life. During the five years I worked with them at Chapel of the Air/Mainstay Ministries, I discovered their fascination with going on a God Hunt.

I also am indebted to SQuire Rushnell and Louise Duart for their *Godwinks* books and movies. These new friends have encouraged me in my desire to actively watch for Godwinks in the midst of my daily routines.

I want to thank Greg Beecham for permission to use his exquisite painting as the cover art for this volume. Greg's reputation as a world renown wildlife artist magnifies his generosity.

I am also grateful for the editorial and design assistance of Rick Lindholtz and On the Tracks Media. This is the third book I have published with Rick's expertise, and certainly not the last.

I am deeply appreciative of the creative mind of C. S. Lewis who first gave the world a lion named Aslan in October 1950 (exactly seventy-one years ago) when the first of the Narnia Chronicles was published.

Finally, I want to thank my best friend and life partner, who accepted my proposal of marriage forty years ago this December. It remains the best Christmas gift I have ever received. Wendy celebrates my love of playing with words and coloring outside the lines.

Aslan made his way into her heart when she was growing up in Mexico. Her hardbound set of the Chronicles of Narnia (given to her by her missionary parents) remain a treasured part of our home library.

Foreword

When you meet Greg Asimakoupoulos, you find a man of compassion with an outreach that comforts with understanding. This was my experience in 1990 in Berkeley, California when Greg and I first met. In recent years I have learned more about his gift of writing poetry and the source of his expression with words inspired. The source is the Christ who stands alongside and brings hope to us – in times of joy and in times of trial.

Greg is a pastor who lives his life with faith. Greg is a poet who brings whimsy into his writing that emerges from who he is and what he believes. In many ways I try to share these characteristics with him. And in particular, I share the discovery of C.S. Lewis, who has given the world the Golden Lion, Aslan, and helped children of all ages to know what it means to have Aslan present in the challenges one meets in life.

And speaking of children, how was I to know way back when Greg and I first met, that his daughter, Kristin, seven years old at the time, would become an intern in Student Ministries during my time as pastor at University Presbyterian Church, Seattle WA? But Aslan knew! And as she sat in our home with other interns over dinner all those many years later, I discovered that her relationship with her dad, and how he had lived and expressed his faith, had inspired her to find her own relationship with Aslan – God, the Father.

Greg and I both treasure the stories of the Oxford poet and novelist who was for each of us our Christian mentor, C.S. Lewis, whose fantasy stories in *The Chronicles of Narnia* introduce Aslan, the Golden Lion, as "swift of foot."[1] In *The Lion, The Witch and The Wardrobe*, when the children first entered Narnia through the wardrobe in the professor's house, Susan upon hearing that they were to meet the Son of the Emperor Beyond the Sea who was "on the move" learns that He is a lion. She asks, "Is he safe?"Mr. Beaver's reply reveals the Lordship of Aslan. "He isn't safe, but he is good."[2] And so the seven novels move forward to spell out how this Lion named Aslan deals with evil – that which is not good.

Greg draws upon the Narnian tales throughout the novels to describe in his poetry how this Good prevails and portrays the role of God/Christ in the world.

---

[1] C.S. Lewis. The Lion, The Witch and The Wardrobe, Geoffrey Bles Ltd, 1950, p. 67

[2] C.S. Lewis. The Lion, The Witch and The Wardrobe, Geoffrey Bles Ltd, 1950, p. 67

I treasure Greg's words in *Aslan, My Protector*:

My King is my protector.
Aslan is His name.
He roars and all is silent,
yet love defines His fame.

Read on to grasp how Greg explains the assurance of Aslan's presence. I like Greg's often humorous insights into the essence of God's presence. Find his poem and read to the end of *When God Speaks*.

When God speaks, I want to hear
against the backdrop of constant distractions.

Amid the din of doing life
in the midst of mounting pressures
and maintaining routines
(all the while pursuing dreams)
I want to sense His presence
and hear the essence of His heart.

Read on to see how Greg brings out the idea of *Godwinks*. I recommend this pastor friend and his poetry to you. You will find meaning. You will find fun. Bravo, Greg!

Earl F. Palmer
Pastor and Author

Introduction

C.S. Lewis was an Oxford don for whom the dawning of faith did not occur until midlife. By his own admission, Lewis crossed the threshold into the Kingdom of God somewhat reluctantly. His conversion (unlike that of the Apostle Paul's) was not instantaneous. Through years of personal research and internal searching, Lewis landed (like Martin Luther) at a place where he took a stand from which he could not be displaced.

Lewis became a prolific apologist in his defense of the Christian faith. His books written in the middle part of the last century continue to be in demand. His Chronicles of Narnia, a collection of metaphoric children's stories, compare the Kingdom of God to a magical kingdom ruled by a lion named Aslan.

My introduction to Aslan was in the form of a play performed by a drama troupe at Seattle Pacific University in the fall of 1974. I had just graduated from this outstanding Christian liberal arts institution and accepted a position in the university relations office. My job found me arranging tours for various performing groups on campus. When the Chancel Players were presented the opportunity to perform *The Lion, the Witch and the Wardrobe* by C. S. Lewis at Expo '74 in Spokane, Washington, I traveled with them.

Never having read any of *The Chronicles of Narnia* in my youth, I was intrigued by the character known as Aslan as presented in the Lewis stories. This lion who served as a Christ-like figure was introduced as powerful. He was good but not safe.

Thirty-five years later I found myself depositing two of my daughters on the campus of Wheaton College in suburban Chicago. The older was pursuing a Master's degree in Counseling Ministries, and the younger was beginning her undergraduate studies in the Conservatory of Music. Having helped them unload their belongings, I went about exploring the campus. I was delighted to discover the Wade Center, named for the founder of ServiceMaster Company.

Within this attractive brick building is contained archived materials and memorabilia related to C.S. Lewis, J.R.R. Tolkien, Dorothy Sayers and G. K. Chesterton. The writing desks of Tolkien and Lewis are displayed along with the wardrobe from Lewis' childhood home, after which his most famous of all the Narnia chronicles is named. I was thrilled by what I saw.

I looked beyond Lewis' wardrobe to see a beautiful, framed painting of Aslan hanging on a wall. It reminded me of the lion sculpture that graced my desk in my office. By now I had come to an informed understanding of Lewis' symbol. The lion was a powerful reminder of an ever-present God who was committed to my wellbeing. I loved the fact that Aslan was capable of making appearances without fanfare. It seemed as though he was always present, even when not visible. He was a means of salvation when all seemed lost.

A dozen years after that self-guided tour of the Wade Center on the campus of Wheaton College, COVID threatened our world. During this time of lockdown and restrictions, as well as fear and anxiety, I noted a number of coincidences that focused my perspective in a heavenly direction. These happenstances reminded me that in spite of being socially distanced, I was not on my own.

My friend SQuire Rushnell refers to such serendipities as Godwinks. In fact, SQuire is the one who coined the term. And during the difficult months of COVID, God, like Aslan, made His presence known at just the right time in unanticipated ways. I began observing Godwinks all around me. I started to sense the hot breath of an uncaged lion on my neck. I knew Aslan was near.

There is a passage of Scripture in the Old Testament in which the protective prowl of our loving God is pictured. Even though he acknowledges times of testing and struggle, in chapter 30 the prophet Isaiah records God's promise to His people to be ever-present in their lives.

18 Yet the LORD longs to be gracious to you;
therefore He will rise up to show you compassion.
For the LORD is a God of justice.
Blessed are all who wait for Him!
19 People of Zion, who live in Jerusalem, you will weep no more. How gracious He will be when you cry for help! As soon as He hears, He will answer you. 20 Although the Lord gives you the bread of adversity and the water of affliction, your teachers will be hidden no more; with your own eyes you will see them. 21 Whether you turn to the right or to the left, your ears will hear a voice behind you, saying, "This is the way; walk in it."

In the very next chapter, the Almighty is pictured as a lion. Could it be that Isaiah 31 is the very chapter that inspired C. S. Lewis to create the character we know as Aslan?

4 As a lion growls,
a great lion over its prey —
and though a whole band of shepherds
is called together against it,
it is not frightened by their shouts
or disturbed by their clamor —
so the LORD Almighty will come down
to do battle on Mount Zion and on its heights.

This volume is a collection of poetry in which the presence of God in our everyday lives is celebrated. Many of the rhymes were written for residents at Covenant Living at the Shores, where I began serving as the fulltime chaplain in 2013. At the end of each poem is a question or prompt designed for contemplation and reflection. At the end of the book are a series of blank pages that encourage the reader to record their own encounters with Aslan.

My hope is that *When God Speaks* will be an interactive journal in which the message found in my poems can result in personal application... that my words will give way to your words and that your awareness of God's presence and God's voice in your daily life will be heightened by what you read and what you do in response.

when God speaks

Listening for Aslan in everyday life

When God Speaks

When God speaks, I want to hear
against the backdrop of constant distractions.

Amid the din of doing life,
in the midst of mounting pressures
and maintaining routines
(all the while pursuing dreams),
I want to sense His presence
and hear the essence of His heart.

When God speaks
I want to know what He is saying.
And even if it means a moratorium from praying
(because my words can often get in the way),
I am willing to be still to know that He is God.

*How might you rearrange your daily routine so as to
remove the distractions of noise from your life?*

Good Not Safe

For goodness' sake, He's good, not safe.
For Heaven's sake, He's God.

This lion in winter
melts the frozen,
treeless,
godless kingdom
with His breath.

In a culture where the holy
has been removed from holidays,
He alone can restore Christmas
to its appropriate place.

His growl is not for the faint of heart.
But it is the welcomed sound of justice
to those who long for his appearing.

His strength offers hope for the weak.
He is a hero to children of all ages.
This King of Narnia is all-powerful.
His impressive mane is but a minor amenity.

Identify examples of how God could be good but not safe.
Does this knowledge undermine your confidence in God's
ability to care for you? Why or why not?

Aslan, My Protector

My King is my protector.
Aslan is His name.
He roars and all is silent,
yet love defines His fame.

When He senses I'm in trouble,
He races to my side.
Like the sun on the Sahara,
His grace can't be denied.

I grab His mane. (He lets me).
His purring drowns my fear.
My enemies are kept at bay
as long as Aslan's near.

Psalm 23 pictures the Lord at work in our lives even while our enemies are present. Read the lyrics of David's most famous poem and imagine Aslan as your companion shepherding you through the shadowlands.

Aslan's Megaphone

Stalked by sorrow in a jungle
of despair and doubt-filled hope,
I hide within the growing shadows
calculating how to cope.

The pain of grief is paralyzing.
Robbed of joy I long to feel,
I'm devoid of all emotions
as I cower where I kneel.

Loneliness is my companion.
No one knows the pain I bear.
How I wish for what eludes me.
One to listen. One to care.

Then I hear a roar that thunders
piercing silence, waking dawn.
And I grasp with understanding
what to do to just hang on.

In these shadowlands of sorrow
where I tremble all alone,
I'm reminded God *is* with me;
Pain is Aslan's megaphone.

C. S. Lewis wrote, "God whispers to us in our pleasures, speaks in our consciences, but shouts in our pains. It is his megaphone to rouse a deaf world." Looking back over your life, when has God used pain and hurtful situations to get your attention?

And He Talks with Me

I come to the garden alone
only to discover that I am not.
Among the dew-drenched roses,
I am aware of One
who walks with me and talks with me.

He reminds me
that I belong to Him.
And the joy we share
(while the dawn is breaking)
is beyond anything I've experienced before.

It's a bond of sweet communion
not easily broken.
It's an uncommon union of friends
bonded for life.
It's a love that will not let me go.

This verse was inspired by the classic hymn "In the Garden." What hymn or worship song comes to mind as you contemplate the personal nature of your relationship with God?

A Godwink Defined

A Godwink is a nod from God.
An eye wink if you will.
It is His way of saying we are loved.
What appears coincidental
is in fact God's grand design.
Be assured our steps are ordered from above.

Godwinks are all around us
if we have the faith to see
how the Lord delights in leaving little hints.
It's so fun to find alignment
in the details of our day
as we dust for where God's left his fingerprints.

What may seem at first as random
is not happenstance at all.
It's how the Lord makes sure we notice Him.
A Godwink is intentional.
It's part of Heaven's plan
to recognize just where God's hand has been.

Looking back on the past week, take time to identify a Godwink in your life or in that of another. How did it make you feel? What did it prompt you to do?

On God's Green Earth

On God's green earth on which we live
we're called to do our part and give
attention to what robs God's world
of dignity and health.

On God's green earth where trash compounds
let's treat our world like holy ground.
Remove the litter others leave.
Recycle when you can.

On God's green earth that we call home,
we can't behave like we're alone.
We share this place with plants and birds,
with animals and fish.

On God's green earth where oceans rise
and rivers flow beneath the skies,
we'd best protect them while we can.
Our water fuels our lives.

On God's green earth where climate change
can cause our weather to be strange,
we can't afford to close our eyes
and blindly just pretend.

On God's green earth, the trees stand tall
and beg for mercy. After all,
if we clear cut and chop at will,
we will in time regret.

On God's green earth we have a choice:
to hear our Great Creator's voice,
or close our ears to what God says
and reap what we have sown.

On God's green earth there still is time.
You do your part and I'll do mine.
Let's take responsibility
and do the best we can.

On God's green earth, I do resolve
that I will be a means to solve
the problems that have plagued our globe,
the planet that we love.

Regardless of your position on climate change, what do
you feel motivated to do as a way of caring for the earth?

In Praise of the Master Artist

Spring is nature's way of saying,
"Death gives way to life."
The dark and cold of winter's grave
gives in to warmth and light.

What once was lifeless, bare and brown
erupts in pink and red.
The yellows of those bulb-born blooms
announce new birth instead.

Yes, spring invites us to resist
the pull of past regrets.
There's glory in a crocus choir.
What's past, we can forget.

"Unwrap the gift of new beginnings!"
Spring shouts loud and clear.
"Use your senses. Praise your Maker!
The Master Artist's here."

In a way, the dawn of each new day is the start of spring.
What will you do today to unwrap the gift God has given
you?

A Wordless Voice

Not in the wind or earthquake.
Not in thunder or a fire.
I heard God speak in a silent wordless voice.
He called through circumstances
in my day to day routines
that align His will with my reluctant choice.

With Elijah I'm reminded
that dramatics aren't God's norm.
The Creator often works in quiet ways.
There are whispers all around us
if we listen with our hearts.
And that wordless voice results in ceaseless praise.

*What does God seem to be whispering to you as you
reflect upon this simple paraphrase of Elijah's encounter
with the living God found in 1 Kings 19?*

God's Leading Man

From a blazing bush that doesn't burn,
God calls His leading man.
But Moses is confused by what he hears.
"Take off your shoes. It's holy ground.
Be still and own My will.
What's now confusing will in time be clear."

God's earth is crammed and every bush
ablaze with majesty.
But most (without a clue) pick blackberries.
The holiness of where we stand
is lost on those who sleep,
content to dream of what old Moses sees.

This rhyme is based on a few lines from an epic poem by Elizabeth Barrett Browning. Why not Google "Aurora Leigh" and read the entirety of her delightful verse?

A Rainbow Reminder

The rainbow is a sacred sign
reminding us that God is kind
and that He'll shepherd us through grief
as sunshine greets the rain.

That rainbow will forever be
God's signature for us to see
our need to trust when doubts arise
and sorrow steals our joy.

Long before the rainbow symbolized the gay rights movement, it was an icon of a covenant-keeping God. When you consider the phrase "as sunshine greets the rain" what recent circumstances in your life found you at the intersection of happiness and hardship? How did God prove faithful?

Sheltering in Grace

When a crisis or virus
might cause us to fear,
we are called to abide and be still.
So we focus our faith
on the Lord's promises,
and are freed from the dread
that we feel.

Abiding in Christ
means to "shelter in grace."
It's the key to remaining alive.
When we make Christ our home
and take root in His love,
we do more than just live.
We will thrive!

*COVID-19 found us "sheltering in place" to limit
exposure to infection. "Sheltering in grace" accomplishes
just the opposite. It exposes us to the infectious life-giving
energy of God's Spirit. Read John 15:1-17.*

COVID Lessons

Remind us, Lord, of lessons learned
when COVID closed down schools
and Sundays found us worshiping through ZOOM.
When dads and mothers worked from home
and masks became the norm.
When headlines held us hostage with their gloom.

We reaffirmed Your faithfulness.
We claimed Your promises.
We rediscovered Church is not a place.
And through it all we realized
we're strong when we are weak,
that all we need is Your amazing grace.

What lessons did you personally learn from surviving the coronavirus? What changes made during the pandemic do you hope will become part of the new normal?

Becoming Like Children

"Become like children," Jesus said.
"Remember who you were.
Wide-eyed with wonder, innocent and shy.
Acknowledging dependence
on that Someone whom you trust.
Accepting more than always asking why?"

Childlike-faith is what we're called to,
Resting in our Father's arms,
Trusting in His vantage point that we can't see.
Making peace with limitations,
while believing dreams come true,
and believing I am loved for being me.

With their arms upraised, small children
reach for Someone whom they love.
Hands aimed Heavenward
convey what's deep inside.
Unconditional affection,
longing to be cradled tight
in those strong inviting arms that beckon wide.

There are shadows on life's highway
that we just cannot avoid.
Unexpected times of darkness hide the sun.
Death and illness. Loss and sorrow.

Doubts that linger through the night.
And those nagging fears
that question what's to come.

Still the shadows offer contrast
give perspective. They provide
a point of reference for God's faithfulness.
In the shadows we are privy
to the promises of grace
that remind us God is with us in our stress.

*Have you ever noticed that King David shifts from
referring to God in the third person to the second person
in verse four of Psalm 23? When the psalmist
acknowledges the "valley of shadows," the LORD
becomes deeply personal to him. What is it about difficult
circumstances that find us relating to God more
intimately?*

The Blessing Bank

Deposits in your blessing bank
are made whenever you give thanks
and gratitude compounds in time
resulting in true wealth.

By counting blessings every day,
your net worth grows along the way.
A grateful heart ignites the joy
that brightens up your world.

For when you add up all that's good,
you focus on the things you should
and realize how blessed you are
in spite of stressful times.

Johnson Oatman wrote the old Gospel hymn "Count Your Blessings." Irving Berlin penned the words to the show tune "Count Your Blessings Instead of Sheep." Don't be sheepish about adding up evidence of God's goodness in your life. What are five things for which you are grateful today?

The Cross is Our Ground Zero

The cross is our Ground Zero
where death gave way to life.
Where love reached out amid a world of terror.
It's where we are reminded of
the peace God longs to give
to every man and woman everywhere.

The cross is our Ground Zero
where history recalls
a day that no one ever can forget.
A day God spoke amid the groans
of pain and misery
while canceling our unpaid moral debt.

The cross is our Ground Zero
where (with gratitude) we bow
acknowledging a sacred sacrifice.
This symbol of our liberty
and freedom from our past
forever calls to mind sin's ugly price.

*As this volume is being written, Americans are somberly
observing the twentieth anniversary of tragic events
associated with September 11. That is when the phrase
"Ground Zero" took on new meaning. Why do you think
"Ground Zero" is an appropriate synonym for the cross?*

A May Prayer

May you discover in this month
that Easter's not a day,
but rather it's a way of life
by which faith learns to play!

May you experience the joy
just knowing Jesus lives!
May you not fear what's still to come
but trust a God who gives.

May you determine to give thanks
for all that's going right.
May you look past another's wrong
so you'll sleep well at night.

May you dust for God's fingerprints
in all that springtime brings:
a flow'ring shrub, a fragrant rose,
the tune a songbird sings.

May you decide to make a friend
of someone you don't know.
May you mend frayed relationships
although you cannot sew.

May you delight in getting fit
by walking every day.
May you eat what is good for you
and chart how much you weigh.

May you take time to talk to God
and then to contemplate
the ways the Lord has answered prayer
with "Yes" & "No" & "Wait!"

May you begin each day this month
by reading from God's Word
and listening expectantly
for what the ancients heard.

May you unwrap each day as if
the present is a gift.
And may God's presence grant you peace
and give your faith a lift.

Looking back on your life, what memories of the month of May do you most cherish?

The Lenten Journey

It's a journey that leads
to the crux of our faith
as we take up our cross day by day.
Acknowledging weakness,
confessing our need
we embrace all God wills as we pray.

Through the desert with Jesus
we walk step by step
well aware of temptations to doubt.
We stumble at times,
but we fall on God's grace
as we puzzle to figure things out.

It's a time for reflection,
for looking inside,
well aware of where this journey ends.
The shadow of death
creeps across what we fear,
but the outcome surprises God's friends.

At the end of the tunnel
there is cause to rejoice.
But for now, we trek on as we wait
for that day we call Easter
when the dawn's early light
will reveal God's on time (never late).

This poem was written during the season of Lent when my friend Doug had undergone heart transplant surgery. The risk of rejection was real. I wanted to encourage him. Who is someone in your life God wants you to encourage today? Write a prayer for them on this page.

A One Word Prayer

I just breathe the name of *Jesus*
when my heart is filled with fear.
And though I cannot see His face,
I know that He is near.

When I whisper *Jesus* softly
I'm admitting I'm in need.
By calling out that precious name,
my stress-bound soul is freed.

It's a one-word prayer I utter
when I'm not sure what to pray.
It's a prayer of sweet surrender
when I'm weary of "my way."

I pray *Jesus* when I'm worried
or when I am depressed.
I say *Jesus* when my mind's confused
or when my life's a mess.

It's a prayer He always answers
as He gives me eyes to see
evidences of His presence
and His tender love for me.

This poem conjures up a Gospel song written by Bill and Gloria Gaither. Perhaps you've sung "There's Just Something About That Name" in church. Did you know that the name Jesus is the Greek form of the Hebrew name Joshua? It means "The Lord is my salvation."

Use the space below to list concerns from which you or someone you love needs saving.

A Reader's Digest of God's Book

The patriarchs and prophets spoke
of Someone who would come
to rid the world of war and hate
so violence would be done.

There was a flood, captivity,
an exodus to save.
A promised land, a virgin birth,
a cross and empty grave.

Came Moses, Sam, a king named Dave,
some minor prophets too.
A 12th man to eleven friends
whose fishing lives were through.

A convert by the name of Paul
who sent a lot of mail.
An exiled pastor on an isle
whose visions leave us pale.

A Reader's Digest of God's Book
reveals the bottom line.
Our moral debt could not be met.
Christ paid it just in time.

God made the world. He loves it, too.
He wants us all to know

He gave us life so we would love.
That's how His Kingdom grows.

This poem attempts to identify the major themes of Scripture. Did you know the third verse of the hymn "How Great Thou Art" reduces the message of the Gospel to thirty-seven words? Why not use the rest of this page to try your hand at summarizing the bottom line message of Christianity? Be creative. Use poetry or prose, bullet points or a diagram.

In Praise of Sighs

A cleansing breath is called a sigh.
It is a tearless whispered cry
that rids the mind of pent-up thoughts
which tend to weigh us down.

A sigh is more than just a groan.
That exhaled air that claims a tone
is like a prayer that needs no words.
It is a holy breath.

A random sigh can purge our angst.
It's worthy of our giving thanks
to One who gave us such a gift.
Be grateful you can sigh!

There is a mountain near to where I live called Mount Si.
It is a constant reminder of why sighing is significant.
Have you ever thought of a sigh as a wordless prayer?

Come up with an acronym for SIGH, such as
Sighing
Is
Groaning
Hopefully

From Heartache to a Timeless Hymn

From heartache to a timeless hymn,
from agony to praise,
the pain of sorrow fills the poets pen.
Both "It Is Well" and "Day by Day"
were birthed in tragedy
as was the treasured lyric "What a Friend."

"Amazing Grace" came from the depths
of Captain Newton's heart
that once had been enslaved by hate and greed.
And Andrae Crouch's "Through it All"
was rooted in despair
as he cried out to God and voiced his need.

Ironically, so many hymns
that draw us near to God
began as wordless groans and whispered sighs.
And yet songwriters filled with faith
And, singed by suffering's flame,
have given us God's truth both sweet and wise.

*The number of well-loved hymns that were birthed
against the backdrop of suffering and hardship is
remarkable. What is one of your favorite hymn stories? If
you don't know any, use your favorite web browser and
simply type in a hymn title and the word "origin."*

Being Mortal

What matters isn't length of life.
It's the quality that counts.
It is celebrating all that God intends.
It's admitting we are dying
while embracing what we love.
It means fully living 'til we reach the end.

It's just not about still breathing.
And it's not just clocking years.
After all, we know eternity awaits.
There is dignity in living
when we honestly admit
that our days are in God's hands (not left to fate).

Being mortal means we're human
and accepting what we are.
It means making peace with illness when it comes.
And while medical advancements
might keep dying folks alive,
we would rather 'dance' until the day we're done.

*"Being Mortal" by Atul Gawande is a popular book that
encourages senior adults to really live life instead of
simply staying alive as long as possible. It is an invitation
to allow God to be the giver and sustainer of life instead of
medical science. Who do you know that might benefit
from a book like that?*

A Blessing for the Bulbs

Within this flower bed shall sleep
these dahlia bulbs where rain shall seep
to irrigate their drowsy dreams
that will at last come true.

This lakeside shoreline where we stand
is not the norm. It's holy land.
A sacred space where soil and sun
combine to create life.

A miracle. It's nothing less
as Mother Nature knits a dress
from skeins of yarn the earth has spun
to clothe the ground with blooms.

Lord, bless these bulbs that they may wake
and be a means to celebrate
the Easter message all year long…
"What's buried still will live!"

*This prayer was written for the flower brigade at the
retirement community where I serve as the fulltime
chaplain. With what phrase or line in the prayer do you
especially relate? Why?*

Where Is God?

So where is God when crazed men kill
their helpless victims sitting still
prepared to worship One who came
to rid our world of hate?

So where is God when children sing
their praises to the King of Kings
and bow their heads as they are told
because He hears their prayers?

So where is God when church folks die
before they have the chance to try
and run away from one intent
on emptying his gun?

So where is God when cynics sneer
and question how could He be near
when evil stalks the innocent
and steals the ones we love?

The answer is "God's everywhere"
observing what we cannot bear
to contemplate or comprehend
because it is so cruel.

God's weeping with us as we grieve.
Our world (unlike what God conceived)
is flawed and broken, filled with rage
and prone to self-destruct.

And yet God has a plan for good
displayed upon a cross of wood
that will in time redeem what's wrong
and vindicate His name.

This poem was birthed by the tragic shooting that took place at a church in Texas in 2017, while adults and children were worshiping.

Because God can handle our questions and our doubts, why not list some of the questions you'd like to ask the Creator about what doesn't make sense in the world?

Waiting for Worship

As I sit in silence
for the service to begin,
I wonder how the risen Christ
will speak to me again.

Will it be the songs we sing?
or in the pastor's prayer?
It just might be her sermon
or a need somebody shares.

Perhaps the Lord will touch my heart
through laughter or a sigh.
Or maybe some distraction
like a newborn's hungry cry.

Whatever means God uses
as He bends my ear His way,
I will listen with expectancy
for there's something He will say.

Photocopy this poem and tuck it in your Bible. Read it to yourself on Sunday morning just before the church service starts. When the service is over, jot down what you think the Holy Spirit was saying to you.

Worship Without End

I don't have to wait for Sunday
to sing praises or to pray.
I can worship God regardless
of the hour or the day.

I don't need a stone cathedral;
I don't need a padded pew.
And though stained windows are quite nice,
most any pane will do.

I enjoy the choir's anthem
and I love the preacher's talk.
But I can sense God's presence
in my car or on a walk.

While it's true I need a Sabbath
and the fellowship of friends,
I'm not limited to Sundays.
It's called worship without end.

*How do you orchestrate a personal worship experience in
your home or workplace? What ingredients are essential
to create an atmosphere where you are apt to sense God's
presence?*

A Cup of Silence

I pour a cup of silence,
my afternoon repast.
A needed brew of emptiness
to pace my race with rats.
Just a simple cup of quiet
to still the noise of grown-up toys
(some call technology).

Silence.

No beepers to turn off.
No faxes to answer.
No cellphone rings to mute.
No deadlines to bury (for now).
Just a sip or two
from this cherished brew.

Silence.

Simon says
(and Garfunkel too)
that silence has its sounds.
I think I would agree.
It's the whisper of a moment
that's tastier than tea.
It's when I hear
the still small voice of God.

Try spending five minutes in total silence. Make note of your impressions on this page.

Morning Prayer

In the twilight of the dawning
as the night gives way to day,
I contemplate Your mercies
and I confidently pray.

You know the fears that haunt me.
You feel the pain I bear.
And in silence as I listen,
I'm reminded that You care.

In the warmth of welcomed daybreak
as the sun's rays light my room,
I'm aware that You are present
and confess my soul's deep wounds.

You know everything about me.
Yet, You love me just the same.
And in quiet meditation
I can hear you call my name.

Margaret Craven wrote "I Heard the Owl Call My Name"a half century ago. In the book's plot, hearing the owl call your name was an indication that your life was nearly over. In the case of hearing the Lord speak your name in that still, small voice, it means life has only just begun.

The Landscape of Thanksgiving

The landscape of thanksgiving
is a picture of Your faithfulness
painted from the palette
of my imperfect situations.

There are times when I feel stretched like a canvas,
have a brush with disaster,
am the victim of a stroke of misfortune
or simply feel unjustly framed.

During those times, Father,
please remind me that You are still at Your easel
using tones and textures I don't really care for
to portray Your grace
against the backdrop of Your glory.

Amid the blustery winds and gray slush
of our wintry world of woes,
Creator God, would You color my life
with the brilliance of Your daily love
and steadfast mercies?

*Can you identify a recent time in your life when you felt
stretched like a canvas? Looking back, did that difficult
experience find you drawing closer to God or pushing
Him away?*

The Trials on the Trail

The trials that define life's trail
are every hiker's bane.
Like fallen limbs across our path,
those trials cause us pain.

They trip us up and make us bleed.
Like undetected stones,
our trials on the trail of life
are hardships we have known.

They knock us flat. And from our knees
we fix our gaze above.
The trials serve to help us see
God's mercy, grace and love.

*Isn't it interesting that the preliminary events in which
athletes compete in order to make the Olympic team are
called trials? Trials are a means of qualifying us for
service in the Kingdom of God. What trials did you face
when you were younger that prepared you for the
"Olympics of Life?"*

The Olympics of Life

The Olympics of life are a constant affair.
There's the balance beam of work and play.
There's wrestling worries and hurdling fear
while pole vaulting problems each day.

There's swimming upstream
'gainst the current of wrong.
There's diving into what needs done.
There's dashing from breakfast to rush-hour grid.
It's a mind-numbing race that we run.

There's the relay of faith where you pass the baton
to both children and grandkids alike.
Yes, we need to be fit as we all exercise
and then trust God with all of our might.

So, Lord, won't you coach us to do what it takes
to finish while doing our best?
Please give us endurance for what comes our way
and then help us to face every test.

*The 2021 Summer Olympic Games were most unusual.
COVID prevented the athletes in Tokyo from competing
before family and friends. The stands were virtually
empty. The athletes competed before their fellow
teammates and their coaches. Does it take the pressure off
you to realize you are competing in life before an audience
of One?*

Seagulls, Fog and Sunsets

Ponderosas, redwoods, cypress
and the sound of rhythmic waves.
Seagulls, fog and sunsets...
such an ambiance You gave this place.
So consistent with Your grace.

Amazing, still so true!
In fact, what I see in nature
fills my mouth with praise for You.

I am moved by Your creation,
prone to wonder, touched with awe;
and because I feel these feelings,
I have a sense of what it means.

Unlike those who were created
by Your verbalized command,
we who bear Your sacred image
alone can understand
who You are and how You love us,
what's in store for such as we.
There's no bird or sea or evergreen
who has a clue of what that means.

How magnificent, dear Father,
that I can contemplate Your truth
and as I drink in what You've made
I am humbled yet mindful of
who I'm called to be.

*Unlike the animals, you were created in the image of God.
As such you have the ability to reflect and meditate on
what the other living beings simply see. Write a prayer in
the space below. Describe how you are impacted by the
beauty of the natural world around you. Thank God for
the gifts of creation.*

A Family Reunion Prayer

Creator of our family tree
(especially the branch called "me")
please let our roots grow deep and strong
so it will stand secure.

From limb to limb our tree has grown.
And, Lord, You've seen how winds have blown.
But by Your grace, strong storms could not
uproot what You preserve.

Allow the blossoms on our tree
to scent our world most fragrantly.
And may the fruit that we will bear
help nourish those You love.

Within the shadow of our tree,
may friends and strangers come to see
the love that binds each one of us
in spite of miles and years.

Family relationships are complicated. Who is someone in your extended family that you find difficult to be around? Are you willing to start praying for that person on a regular basis? Are you willing to ask the Lord to change your attitude toward that individual?

The Lord's Prayer (a poetic paraphrase)

Our Father in Heaven, we pause now to pray,
enveloped by pressures on earth.
We struggle to trust You when life hems us in
or when critics question our worth.

We honor Your name,
Elohim, Adonai,
El Shaddai, Tzevaot, Yahweh, too.
Most Holy, Almighty, Compassionate One,
You are just, ever faithful and true.

We welcome Your Kingdom,
Your Highness, we're Yours,
surrendered to what You allow.
Your will is what matters for You know what's best.
So we (in humility) bow.

May You reign supremely in Heaven and here
accomplishing what You deem best.
A Kingdom of kindness, forgiveness and love,
of order, rich beauty and rest.

We pray that this day we'll be nourished with food,
by our friendships, the arts and Your Word.
Our bodies and spirits rely on Your grace
lest our focus on Truth becomes blurred.

Forgive us our failures, O Father, we pray.
We stumble so often, it seems.
Our willful desires breed actions that wound
while exposing our self-centered schemes.

But only forgive us, dear Father, we pray,
as we are inclined to forgive
the ones who have wronged us. May we offer grace
even though it's so hard to give.

Temptations that threaten our lives loom ahead.
Like landmines they can't be perceived.
Please, Father, protect us and guard us from harm
and the evil that seeks to deceive.

Deliver us daily from sin's unseen traps
that trip up those blind to their pride.
Admitting our weakness, we ask for Your help.
God of mercy, in You we confide.

For Yours is the Kingdom to which we belong.
It's glory, dominion and might
defy understanding and can't be explained
by the smartest (no matter how bright).

By faith we submit to Your unending reign.
As Your children we live quite assured
that what You intend, loving Father, is good.
And that what we've just prayed has been heard.
Amen.

Do you find the familiarity of the Lord's Prayer monotonous, or do the predictable words and phrases provide you a sense of comfort and connection? What accounts for the way you feel?

Christianity 101

Unlike Muslims, Jews or Sikhs,
what makes Christ-followers unique
is their belief there's just one way
that we can get to God.

And though that may seem strange to some,
just think of dialing 9-1-1.
When you're in need, there's just one call
that's sure to get you help.

For God so loved the world, He came
to be a human with a name,
to take the rap for what we've done
and take away our guilt.

While some think you can earn your way,
that's not what you'll hear Christians say.
They are convinced that what Christ
did is all that is required.

So when it all is said and done,
what matters most is that God's Son
was born and died and came to life
that we might know we're loved.

Christianity is sometimes criticized as being intolerant and exclusive because Jesus claimed to be the "only way" to God. Does calling 9-1-1 to get help in saving a life provide a metaphor you can use next time you are challenged with Jesus' words?

God is Like My iPhone

I AM is like my iPhone.
God is with me wherever I go.
Just like my smart phone,
He gives me direction when I'm lost.
His vast knowledge is limitless.
He fills my life with a source of music.
He wakes me each morning.
He is a source of light in the darkness.
His memory exceeds mine.
With Him I can deposit my concerns
and withdraw His grace immediately.
He always has time for me.
He connects me with those I need
and those who need me.
He provides me with pictures
of people and places
that define His plan for my life.
He allows me to take a selfie
in order to focus on just how blessed
I am.

*What are features of your smartphone that you can't
imagine living without? How do you use your
smartphone as a means of spending time with the Lord or
serving others on God's behalf?*

Life is Precious

Life is precious, sacred, blest
from the womb to final rest.
God is in a child's first breath,
or a grandpa facing death.

Special needs autistic son,
Crippled daughter who can't run.
Those impaired in speech or sight,
Those whose hearing isn't right.

Those who can't recall their name,
Those with damage to their brain.
Those in prison, addicts too,
Those who think their options few.

Each life matters. Each has worth.
Everyone on God's green earth.
Life is precious, sacred, blest
from the womb to final rest.

*In Matthew 25 Jesus relates a parable to his disciples
referencing the "day of judgment." He suggests that those
who lovingly care for individuals in need are essentially
caring for Him. With that in mind, how can you care for
"Jesus" today? Who comes to mind? What could you do
as unto the Lord?*

Friended by God

God friended me through Facebook.
He clicked "love" instead of "like."
I was humbled by the fact He knew my name.
And what is more, God commented
below what I had shared.
He posted on my wall "I feel your pain."

God tagged me in a photograph
of Jesus on the cross.
I didn't understand the reason why.
But then the Lord reminded me
He hung there for my sin,
that I was on His mind the day He died.

I have memories with the Lord of Life
the day He wore my crown.
Good Friday is our anniversary.
For that is when a holy God
befriended me in love
just as I am, without a single plea.

*Ever since Facebook was invented by a couple of college
students at Harvard, it has become an indispensable part
of people's lives. It allows for former classmates, friends
and family to connect on a regular basis. When we post a
photo or a comment, we look to see if someone has "liked"
what we've put up. What does God "like" that others
don't seem to notice?*

Adam's Mark

Adam's mark. The Creator's touch.
The soul's divine tattoo.
It's an image that enables Eden's children
to imagine and create.

It is what animates all who paint or sketch
and is reflected on their canvases and prints.
It is the hand of God upon the Garden prince
that has touched you with desire
to make your mark upon the world
and help it see the Light.

*According to the Book of Genesis, Adam was given the
privilege of naming the animals in Eden. That was one
tangible way he left his mark. What are tangible ways you
can leave your mark on the world? If this question seems
difficult to answer, why not use this page to jot down
unique interests and abilities you have? Can you name
them?*

The Lord is My Musher

The Lord is my musher.
I'm part of His team.
He makes sure I take time to rest.
At checkpoints He feeds me
and offers me drink.
No wonder I give Him my best.

O'er trails of His leading,
He coaxes me on.
And when shadows darken my way,
I will not be fearful
for He is in charge.
Contented, I want to obey.

My bowl overflows
with the proof of His care.
My weary bones welcome His touch.
And as I draw near
to the end of my race,
He whispers I'm loved very much.

Yes, goodness and mercy
both bark at my heels.
They'll follow me all the way home.
And when I have reached
the burl arch of my life,
I know God will call me His own.

*The Iditarod Sled Dog Race commemorates the famous
Serum Run of 1925, when mushers and sled dogs saved
the lives of the residents of Nome, Alaska.*

*Ever since 1973, the annual Iditarod has concluded under
the "burl arch" on front Street in the famed Gold Rush
town. The musher of a dog team is like the shepherd of a
flock of sheep. Both a musher and a shepherd take
responsibility for those under their care. How does God
care for you daily? Use this page to document evidences
of His care.*

Life is Like a Round of Golf

Life is like a round of golf.
It's a walk with valued friends.
It tests your skill and finds you yelling "Fore!"
The bunkers and the hazards
try your patience and your faith
as you anticipate your final score.

You're grateful for a Mulligan
when you (at times) mess up.
Like "breakfast balls" the Good Lord offers grace.
Perfection is elusive,
but you give it your best shot
in hopes you'll reach your dream and card an ace.

And when you've played your final round
and reach the 19th hole,
you calculate what matters most of all:
Your family and your colleagues
and the memories you made
while chasing after that white dimpled ball.

*The 23rd Psalm is the most well-known of all the hymns
in Israel's ancient hymnbook. This is an attempt to
personalize it for those who love to chase a little white ball
around "green pastures." Who is someone you love who
loves golf? With which stanza do you think they would
most relate?*

Night Has Dissolved into Day

The past has given way to the present.
Today is just that. It is a gift!
I'm bathed in the warmth and beauty of a sunrise.
The dawn's early light calls to mind much more
than our national anthem.
The glow of this new morning flags my attention
and awakens my faith.
A night of rest has refreshed my soul
and distanced my weary mind
from the stalking doubts of yesterday.
With the sunrise I'm reminded of a powerful truth...
"This is the day the Lord has made.
I can rejoice and be glad in it!"

Using the space below, make a list of things you can do that will help you to make the most of God's gift called "today."

Hawaiian 23rd Psalm

The Lord is my oarsman.
He steers my canoe
and paddles me safely to shore.
He whispers *aloha* and calls me by name
while pointing to what lies in store.

The palm trees that sway
and the tropical breeze
picture all that awaits when I die.
Such beauty, refreshment,
contentment and peace.
And pleasure that money can't buy.

And though I may falter, and fall on my face,
the Lord walks with me in the sand.
His goodness surrounds me and steadies my step.
His mercy will help me to stand.

He bids me draw close,
drapes a lei round my neck
and tells me I've nothing to fear.
"I'll never forsake you.
I'll always provide
and I promise I'll always be near."

Here's another example of paraphrasing Psalm 23 in a contemporary context. Those who translate the Bible in unwritten languages are tasked with the challenge of identifying redemptive analogies. Who is someone involved in Bible translation that you know? How can you pray for them?

The Game of Life

The game of Life can be quite fun
until (at last) it's finally done.
And then when we've had one last turn
it all goes in the box.

Much like Monopoly is played
we buy and sell and sometimes trade.
And even when we've earned a lot,
it goes back in the box.

Like Scattergories and Taboo,
life's filled with Risk for me and you.
We can be Sorry when the pieces
go back in the box.

It's Trivial Pursuit at best.
We haven't got a Clue unless
we get a Yahtzee just before
it goes back in the box.

But life is more than just a game
and that is why the Savior came
so we can know the final score
before we're in a box.

When you were a kid what was your family's favorite board game? What special memories do you have of game nights? In the "Game of Life" the concept of all the pieces going back in the box is a sobering one. What do you need to take care of before your "Game" is over?

The Gospel According to Spring

It was as if somebody died.
For three months we have grieved.
We've mourned for flowers dead and gone
and trees that lost their leaves.

The gloom of winter gripped our hearts
as Boston caved to snow.
Our frozen lawns were lifeless brown.
Our plants refused to grow.

Death's shadow fell across the land.
We sorrowed for our loss.
The toll of winter just won't quit
exacting quite a cost.

But come this weekend life bursts forth
from winter's icy grave.
Spring is creation's metaphor
for One who came to save.

Spring pictures resurrection truth.
Yes, death has been defeated
because God's plan to prove His love
outrageously succeeded.

Those who live in the Midwest experience four distinct seasons. The transition from winter to spring is noteworthy. It is nature's way of preaching an Easter sermon. What was a memorable Easter in your life? Did it relate to a church service? Or did it have to do with a family gathering?

On Spiritual Wellness

I've come to see that wellness
is much more than being fit.
A healthy body needs a healthy soul.
And while dieting and exercise
can do a body good,
a person really needs a higher goal.

It's great to run a marathon
or jog five times a week,
but running after peace has merit, too.
And while walking before supper
can burn dreaded calories,
a daily walk with God is good for you.

To bend and flex has merit.
So, we strive to stay in shape.
As we age, we must maintain agility.
But God also wants to stretch us
to expand our usefulness.
It's His will that we become all we can be.

Yes, our bodies are a temple
that deserve refurbishment
lest through disrepair they start to fall apart.
But a temple's just a building
if it's just an empty shell.
So let's exercise our souls and guard our hearts.

Someone has said somewhat sarcastically, "Physically fit people die healthier!" While eating healthy and getting exercise are important disciplines, some have made physical fitness a religion. What exercises do you need to incorporate into your daily regimen to improve your spiritual health?

A Tribute to Hospice Nurses

When death knocks and life's clock
ticks in slow motion,
it's easy to tell the time.
But it's difficult to accept what it says.

That's when hospice nurses
make their way
to the line of scrimmage
for the final minutes of the game.

They know that beating the opponent
isn't possible
and yet they make the most
of the little time that's left.

Tackling whatever is necessary
they clear the way so that you can
make your way into the end zone
with head held high
and faith clutched tightly to your chest.

They're the best
(though they are often the unsung).
They are heroes of the dying
(and those living who stand watch).
They are angels of mercy, shepherds of grace,
guardians of dignity
and servants of the most high God.

Do you know any hospice nurses or chaplains? Consider making a photocopy of this poem and sending it to them, enclosed in a greeting card.

Are you aware of anyone receiving hospice care as death approaches? Spend time praying for them, and the medical staff who care for them.

God's Masterpiece

With palette, paint and brush in hand,
the Artist has at his command,
the simple tools by which He will
create a masterpiece.

But at the start you'd never know
what one day will be best-of-show
is nothing more than colored globs
that seem like a mistake.

"Forget it!" one voice quickly cries.
"Don't waste your time!" another sighs.
"There's just no way that what He's done
will ever be acclaimed."

The Artist hears but doesn't turn.
He knows that those who scoff might learn
that what they see as random strokes
are priceless art indeed.

But from the start there is no way
to tell what will emerge one day
and so the Artist's infant work
is often mocked and tossed.

And when it is the Artist grieves
for what in love His mind conceived
will never be the work of art
He knew would bless a home.

And all because uncultured folks
who thought His masterpiece a joke
are free to wreck what is not theirs
and judge the Artist wrong.

Is that the freedom wars have won?
Where works of art are left undone
because it's thought until they're framed
they're free to be destroyed?

May God forbid! May He paint on
without the claims that He is wrong.
For every life's a masterpiece
the moment He begins.

*Read Psalm 139. How do those verses illustrate God's
role as an artist? What verses in this poignant psalm
portray your life as a masterpiece? If you were to ask God
to "search you inside and out" what would the Creator
expose?*

Image Bearers

Creation is the canvas on which God's artistic brush
reflects His very image as it prompts a holy hush.
Majestic elk and graceful swans, the agile antelope
are spiritual to look at, as are Rocky Mountain goats.

God woos us through the caribou,
the arctic fox and owl,
a black bear shimmying a tree, a lion on the prowl.
A beaver in a mountain stream creatively survives.
And in the secret life of bees,
there's order in the hive.

A fuzzy worm transforms itself to be a butterfly.
A pair of circling eagles dance
against the azure sky.
Each creature boasts God's fingerprints.
Astounding symmetry.
Amazing strength. Minute details. It's all a mystery.

But it's not only in the beast we see the Artist's art.
It's in the creativity that occupies our heart.
The painter, sculptor, novelist,
photographer and poet
are bearers of Divine mystique.
And in our hearts, we know it.

The animal kingdom is evidence of the Creator's creativity. In creatures large and small, God reveals His penchant for detail. What details of your life are you inclined to forget that your Heavenly Father knows about?

Longing for Retreat

There's a place where God's grace
tastes refreshingly cool,
like a gurgling brook in the woods.
It's a place that you dream of
when life hems you in
with its pressures, its oughts and its shoulds.

It's a place where contentment comes easy.
Where quiet like a quilt calms your sleep.
Where you're mindful of nature
and relaxed about clothes.
Where the friends that you make are for keeps.

It's a place reminiscent of Heaven.
Where feasting is more than good food.
Where worship has meaning
and the Lord seems more real
than you ever expected He could.

It's a place where your heart longs to move to,
more spacious than you'll ever own.
A place that is priceless
and worth every cent.
It's a place where your heart feels at home.

Some families are fortunate enough to have a vacation cottage. Other families have a traditional campsite or hotel in a certain location they enjoy. Some look forward to going to the same church camp each year. Where did you and your family go?

A God for All Seasons

In every season of my days
when I am stressed or prone to praise,
I'll hope in God's deliberate ways
to guide me through life's mazes.

When joy explodes within my mind
and faith seems easy (almost blind),
I'll worship Him in whom I find
a constant true companion.

When skeptics shake my confidence
and cause my faith to sigh and wince,
I'll look for Heaven's righteous Prince
to help me doubt my doubting.

When health declines and leaves me ill
and pain persists in spite of pills,
I'll trust my Father's perfect will,
embracing what's before me.

When worry robs what God intends
to fill my heart when my life ends,
I'll count on Him to be my friend
and give me grace for dying.

Read James 1:17. It's been said, "The only thing that remains constant in life is change." While that hyperbole communicates the constancy of change in our lives, it overlooks the fact that the Lord we worship is "the same yesterday, today and forever."

Longing for Home

Father God,
deep within
I long for a place to call home.
A sanctuary of safety.
A place of rest.
A nest where I am known
and loved.
A place where I am free.
Like a bird on the wing,
I crave a place to perch and sing
where,
sheltered from the world's cold wind,
I find the means to cope.
And what I hope for(I believe)
is in Your open arms.

*You likely have heard the expression, "Home is where the
heart is!" From the time we are children, we long for a
place of belonging. It's a place where we can feel accepted
just as we are. How is the heart of God that kind of place?*

The Joy's in the Climb

It's not on the summit
where faith tends to grow.
We learn how to trust
in the valley below.

The trek is what matters.
The joy's in the climb
as we practice God's presence
one day at a time.

Christian singer/composer Michael Card is known for his song "Joy in the Journey." What song titles can you think of that celebrate the priceless treasure that is today? Feel free to use the empty space on this page to jot down the songs that come to mind.

Giants in the Land

It's a desert that I'm dealing with
(this land of barren waste)
where I daily make a choice to stay "the call."

It's a wilderness, that's all.
The promised land of discipleship
is far from milk and honey anymore.

Sweet Jesus, there are giants in the land.
The hot breath of prowling cougars singes my hope.
Power-hungry jackals stalk my joy.
Wolves, clothed like sheep, steal my trust.
The heat's always on in this land of shadows.
I'm tired.
I'm thirsty.
I'm tempted to quit.
It's about all I can take.

I'm aware of my enemies' presence.
But where are the green pastures and still waters?
Those succulent Egyptian melons
sure would taste good right now.
I could go for some garlics and leeks.
Lord, my resilience is weak.
And in the midst of the wilderness,
I am hoping You will find me.

After 400 years of inhumane treatment in Egypt, the children of Israel were tempted to forget God's promise of a better life for the sake of familiar foods that represented the best of a bad situation. It is still true today. What are the "leeks and garlics" that tempt you to return to your Egyptian bondage?

A Wardrobe in Disguise

"It won't be long now,"
you said with a smile,
your emotions under control.
And I marveled at your calm.
But when you got that call that said
all had been done (and all was not enough),
didn't it take a while for your ready smile
to find your face again?

You are never quite ready
for the end to come, are you?
Even when you've had wind of the end
for a while.

When you finally face that familiar face
inside that greedy box,
your resignation to what you thought
you were prepared for
quickly bolts out the door,
leaving you alone with the lonely truth
that life will never, ever, really be the same.

But as Paul Harvey was wont to say...
"And now for the rest of the story!"

Death's only glory is that overpriced coffin
in which it thinks it's sealed our fate

(and that of those we loved).
But Death forgets its box is but a wardrobe
through which the Risen Lion leads us
(and all those with faith)
into the Land of Narnia
where Death
(even if it could be remembered)
would only be a bad dream.

Long live, Aslan! Deep be Your peace!

In "The Lion, the Witch and the Wardrobe," the author invites us to enter the land of Narnia through an old-fashioned bedroom wardrobe. That standing wooden box is the means by which a new world is experienced. Have you ever thought of a casket as a wardrobe? For the Christian, a simple pine box is a time-capsule to eternal life. If you have never read the classic story by C. S. Lewis, why not commit to reading it this year?

In the space below, list the names of those family members and friends who trusted Christ as their only hope in death and now are waiting for you to join them in the actual "Narnia."

The Ubiquitous Cross

A Godwink? Maybe!
You decide.
The cross on which
my Savior died
keeps showing up.
It's here. It's there.
It's everywhere I look.

A sidewalk crack.
A window frame.
A door design.
It's like a game.
God hides the cross.
I seek to find
the symbol of His grace.

The trail on which
I often walk
revealed some wood
amid the rocks.
A crucifix. God's gift to me.
A most amazing find!

Why not look for the ultimate symbol of God's grace in everyday places as you go about your everyday life today? When you see the sign of the cross, say "Thank you for Jesus!"

Use the space below to record places where you find the shape of the cross unexpectedly.

The Creator Speaks

In nature the creator speaks.
A gurgling brook or mountain creek
are all he needs to bend my ear
so I can hear his voice.

The wind swept prairies boasting grain
or northwest forests drenched in rain
are means by which God whispers
"I'm the source of all that lives!"

The seacoast with its deafening waves,
the echoes of a pitch-black cave
are sounds that point to One who spoke
and said "Let there be life!"

On mountain summits cloaked with snow
or in the desert sands below
creation sings God's majesty
and bids me join the song...
"Praise to the Lord, the Almighty, the King of
creation..."

Listening for God to speak is a daily challenge. There are
lots of distractions and noises that can drown out God's
voice. But we tend to hear what we are listening for.

How Autumn Leaves Me

It's amazing, God,
how autumn leaves me
awed by Your majesty.
There's a bite in the air
that nips at the leaves
that blush orange and red
from the nibbles of the night.

Without warning
they fall to the ground
and carpet the earth with their color.
There is every reason
to reap the blessings You've sown in my life
and offer the bounty of my grateful heart to You.

*Have you ever made note of the fact that autumn begins
with "awe?" What is it about the season of fall that you
most appreciate? Even though you may not be artistic,
try your hand at sketching a maple leaf in the space
below. Inside the leaf, list words that spell out the
awesome things you enjoy during autumn.*

I Prayed for You Today

Even though I wasn't sure
exactly what to say,
I talked to God and spoke your name.
I prayed for you today.

I asked the Lord to give you strength,
to calm you from your stress,
to free you from the things you fear
and bathe your mind with rest.

I asked the Lord to help you
in the uphill days to come.
I asked our precious loving God
to complete what He's begun.

He whispered in the quiet
and He filled my heart with peace.
He said that you are deeply loved
and that His love won't cease.

Even though you might not know exactly how to pray for
them, who are the people about whom you are concerned?
List their names below.

Awaiting King Aslan's Return

Caught in the traffic of daily distresses,
trapped in routines that have lost their appeal,
weary of holding to dreams that allure us,
maranatha, King Aslan, we await Your return.

Jaded by broken commitments and losses,
reeling from setbacks that robbed our reserves,
fearing the words of a doctor's announcement,
maranatha, King Aslan, we await Your return.

Troubled by cultural trends that are godless,
doubting decisions the courts deem as fair,
haunted by laughter that mocks human kindness,
maranatha, King Aslan, we await Your return.

Longing for what You intended in Eden,
hoping for meaning beyond what we see,
looking for ultimate justice and mercy,
maranatha, King Aslan, we await Your return.

*Using the space below, write a brief prayer conveying
what you long to see made right in this imperfect world of
ours.*

The Edge of Adventure

When God brings you to the edge
you think there's not much cause to hope.
It is clear that there's a drop off.
There's no path and you've no rope.

If you jumped, you wouldn't make it.
Kinda looks like life is through.
But if you'll just be patient,
God, in time, will rescue you

Such occasions call for trusting
and that goes against our grain.
We don't like what faith requires;
no firm answers, sometimes pain.

All the same God can be trusted.
He won't leave you on the brink.
Don't put all your stock in feelings
or in what (at times) you think.

Put your weight on what God's promised.
Lean on Him and do not fear.
Though it's scary where you're standing,
ask for courage. God is near.

The BeFrienders Ministry is an organization that trains pastors, chaplains and laypersons in the art of listening. BeFrienders exists to help people going through life changes by offering companionship and the promise of God's presence. The foundational premise claims that "God is present." How would your attitude toward life change if you began each day convinced that God is present?

Aslan Rules

In the jungle,
the mighty jungle
of a world spinning out of control,
the Lion doesn't sleep tonight
or at any time.

This Lion watches from his perch.
His focused gaze sees all.
His clawed paws
rest ready to render justice
when required.

In the jungle,
the mighty jungle,
where what is right
is left out of the equation,
Aslan rules.

"In the Jungle, the Mighty Jungle" became a smash hit record for The Tokens in 1961. How does the world of today seem like a mighty jungle to you? Who seems to be sleeping and unaware of the chaos?

The Lion King

The shape of things to come
in the Kingdom of His reign
is only foreshadowed here on earth.

In the circle of life
hakuna matata squares with
what the Bible teaches.
We are encouraged not to worry
because the King is in control.

Even when the King's subjects
are subjected to unfair outcomes
and unjust treatment,
He who reigns still rules.

"The Lion King" is a Broadway show as well as an animated movie. Through it we learned the phrase hakuna matata which means "don't worry!" What is a source of anxiety and fear in your life right now that is too big for you to carry alone? Why not give it to the One who is aware of your need and cares more than you know?

Let's Hear it for Poetry!

There are times you need a poem
to express the pain inside.
Words fall short as feelings lengthen.
Plus, in sorrow, thoughts can lie.

Poets have a way of sifting
through the rubble of our grief.
In their lyrical expressions,
mourners often find relief.

When they sense God's holy presence
and are silenced by His grace,
they're amazed how poets' brushes
can portray His unseen face.

And when joy exceeds description
at a wedding or a birth,
there is nothing like a poem
to convey life's deepest mirth.

Ever noticed just how often
someone quotes some poetry?
In an ocean of emotion,
rhyming verses calm the sea.

So when asked if I'm a poet,
I don't wince or hang my head.
I can't think of a vocation
that I'd rather claim instead.

*It's your turn to try your hand at writing a poem. It can
be one that follows a prescribed meter, one that rhymes, or
what is often referred to as blank verse. Use the space on
this page to express your feelings and paint a picture
using descriptive words, phrases, and similes.*

I Heard God Speak

I read God's Word.
I heard Him speak.
I'd recognize that familiar voice
anywhere.

In the pages of humanity's history,
Israel's genealogy,
a shepherd's poetry,
a prophet's prediction,
a wise king's journal,
a lover's diary,
a tax collector's ledger,
a physician's travelogue,
an apostle's correspondence,
and a disciple's vision
the living God got my attention.

His voice (though inaudible)
is unmistakable.
And the words I hear
(though not always welcomed)
communicate caution,
offer guidance,
check my pride,
inspire new ideas,
silence my fears,
reprimand my disobedience
and whisper His love.

God's voice is most often heard through God's Word. How often do you read the Bible? What is your approach? When is it most fulfilling? How might you alter where and when you read the Scripture?

Poets are God's Artists

Poets are God's artists.
With pen in hand they sketch the world
with ink and words and metaphors.
They do what they adore.
In the process they draw a door to truth
for those who seek to knock.

Poets, you see, are finders
who are not content to keep
their treasures to themselves.
They must express what they confess to see.
It's a passion that burns within them.

Awake to life (their hearts afire),
poets pray on paper.
They are keepers of the flame
that blazes in the soul of humankind.

You may not consider yourself a poet, but you know the power of the written word. Perhaps you relate to the sentiment of Dawson Trotman (the founder of the Navigators) who once observed, "Thoughts untangle and make more sense when they pass through articulating fingertips."

Listening for Aslan

A field guide for a spiritual safari

Listening for Aslan

Take a few minutes to look back at what took place today.

Who did you interact with?

What insights did you glean from that interaction?

What took place over the course of the day that you hadn't anticipated?

When were you most aware of God's presence today?

On what passage of Scripture did you read and reflect?

What do you think the Lord was attempting to say to you?

How do you intend to apply what you heard?

If you were to convey your candid feelings to God, what would you say?

Use the next several pages to record your spiritual safari.

About the Author

Greg Asimakoupoulos is an ordained minister with The Evangelical Covenant Church, having served congregations in California, Illinois and Washington State. Since 2013 he has served as the fulltime chaplain at *Covenant Living at the Shores*, a retirement community in suburban Seattle.

Greg is the author of fourteen books and is a frequent contributor to various Christian periodicals. He also writes a regular column for three newspapers.

Greg and his wife Wendy have three grown daughters and two granddaughters. They live on Mercer Island where there are frequent Aslan sightings.

About the Artist

The lion painting on the cover of this book is called *The Warrior King*. The artist is Greg Beecham. This internationally acclaimed wildlife artist has been putting paint to canvas for more than forty years.

Greg's father Tom Beecham was a celebrated illustrator and artist from whom the younger Beecham drew inspiration. Early in his life Greg B discovered that he had been gifted by God with a talent not unlike that of his famous father.

Greg A first met Greg B in 1979 after joining the pastoral staff of a neighborhood church in Seattle. Greg B and his wife Lu had joined the congregation a few months before. He had recently completed his service with the Navy and begun a career as a freelance book illustrator.

Because Greg A and Greg B were about the same age and shared similar interests, a friendship developed. Itwas clear that Greg B's true passion (like his father's) was wildlife art. It was inspiring for Greg A to watch his friend experience initial success and acceptance in the field of his true calling.

Over the past four decades, Gregs A and B have maintained contact and dreamed of collaborating on a project together. This book, with *The Warrior King* as its cover art, is a small step in that direction.

Greg Beecham's amazing talent can be viewed at his website: gbeecham.work

For additional resources to assist you on your own spiritual safari, check out these books:

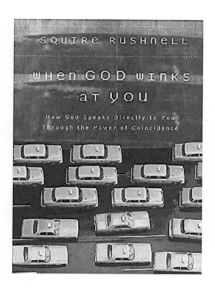

*When God Winks at You:
How God Speaks
Directly to You Through the
Power of Coincidence*
by SQuire Rushnell
Thomas Nelson Publishers

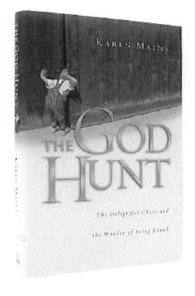

*The God Hunt:
The Delightful Chase and
the Wonder of Being Found*
by Karen Mains
available through
Mainstay Resources